# BEAST

# MERIDIAN

Vanessa Angélica Villarreal

Book Cover Design: Natalie Eilbert
Book Interior Design: Sarah Gzemski

Published by Noemi Press, Inc. A Nonprofit Literary Organization.
www.noemipress.org.

# BEAST

## MERIDIAN

Vanessa Angélica Villarreal

*When the settler seeks to describe the native fully in exact terms, he constantly refers to the bestiary.*

Frantz Fanon

*Bridges span liminal (threshold) spaces between worlds, spaces I call nepantla, a Nahuatl word meaning tierra entre medio. Transformations occur in this in-between space, an unstable, unpredictable, precarious, always-in-transition space lacking clear boundaries. Nepantla es tierra desconocida, and living in this liminal zone means being in a constant state of displacement ...*

Gloria Anzaldúa

*in memory of Angelica Lopez, Carmen Lopez, Guadalupe y Mario Sanchez, y Carlos Lopez*

for ANGELICA
*an elegy*

Diagnosed, your hands became my bread
& we ate them—

& the hair flew off your head & wove
great red nests

*selah*    for us women

your black cervix rot my first egg drop
& so we hatched myself—

this is how we said you would survive:

# TABLE OF CONTENTS

AN ILLNESS OF PINES

# MALINCHE

I find the victims in the valley    I hunt the wilderness in myself    I stalk my prey through myself    let hornets hive my womb    I am born fragrant stars    and make planets of my body    I noble the old people    I make victim the valley I make mountains kneel in myself    I eat a crown of lead    make him an air

I unearth the noble
young women I cleave
violence into ourself
valley the victim she
valley it is my own sun
valley it is my sun
the wilderness in
to the kingdom I am
new world I entomb
grow mild flowers
betrayed nation I

victim I make valleys of
white the wilderness take
I victim the gods in the
is myself victim in the
I stalk my victim in the
people I hunt my hunter
myself I open my illness
cleaved by the old and
elders in the valley and
of their teeth I birth a
fill with hunted the

wilderness is myself my illness led us to this see my braid the poisoned river and the lost tongues I walk as night I carry the child of the noble cause I make my victim my nation in the valley I hunt the wilderness in myself stalk the tall grasses I am she who betrays blood for a little bit of kingdom

# CROSSOVER ALBUM

SIDE A. IT IS almost all gone. Remains:

canicas in the grass    futbol dim from the

trailer    salgasen a la chingada    or clean

the beans of stones    doll car parked

among onions    cuna de lobos    milanesa

con arroz    siempre en domingo    then

outside botas share Winston smoke    a

crush of Bud Lite cans    we chase-the-gallo

then race-to-the-end    le voy a decir a tu

papá    trucks wall in our citrus laughter

ringing bright lavender dusk    SIDE B. marbles again this time    milkopaled

ringing    southwestern bell    another faraway

family member    dead    and I'm turning mala

huerca hechada a perder    no after no    a knot

good ache pulls up a sun in me    bisabuela

Carmelita cabeceando during the rosary    for the

prima long-missing    the valley a thrash wildrosed

and so the women knit basil    into rosaries purify

us    with un huevo crack    its melancholy galaxy

into a glass    still fail to mute that    lowsung bud

between our serious inherited pompis    swaying

down a child    and the river will call    that baby

its own    as it also calls back    the dying body

an iterating loop of escape and return    of

mothers and work    of fathers and violence


prima emerges from the apple fields    a citizen in

her belly    I am returned to beg back    this

amber music   written in me

†

† IN THE flooded city    your head    will stay below water    blonde pines    the country club
calls a meeting    to draw lines around    you    Weiner's clothes and used domestic cars
barbacoa and dollar store virgins    god bless the Family Lexus    already so tight-gated    the entry code your
sponge your doubled tongue so wound    still festers into childbearing    reported in your own
country    you still race baby    to the same dead-end    hard missing from    the rio grande valley
night    still giving birth to you    the hipdeep cumbias    blast from pickups    filled with your
pasts    your people endless    chambeando jalando    that distance    heavy fades the star stories
in your skin    makes a weapon    of forgetting    makes a knife your grammar-groomed tongue

our dead                                 only yesterday                              a petal

     now curled           into burnt bone              their ash our flour

we ascend their spirit                           into the design              a fragrant magic

          an ever-distancing              orbit              a chorus I am losing

     grasp                 of   their particular   moons                 fail

          to record              that          their perfect feet              ever graced

this earth                              their ghost                              a homing

signal               constellated

                                             in corn husk    new bone

what did you make:               of their sacrifice?
                                 of their tender impossible longing?
                                 of their unbearable silence?
                                 of their witness?

                                 each try               a permanent loss

# TIME, TWO-HEADED: CORPUS CHRISTI, 1984

In this photo     mami y papi     are too young
to ignore          the gulf          that will swell
between them    the pristine water unrolling
into     their sanded bodies     racking toward
ruin          some brunette          shadow passes
overhead          casts doubt     one of   us
          had to falter,               one of us
          had to  hazard           the ocean
mothering its dead


just as     waves gather from chaos    so does


a spirit          find absence          a dull quiet
pulled ever
                    apart            from peace

her    scalloped    spine      carries    us:
horsemother, draped on sofa, dull tv light
a blued pitch      no craving      her open
mouthed sleep      her  workthick nurture
so steady hipped      I brush cigarette ash
from the sofa cushion  forever flattened by
her weary weight      and lift      that
strange angel    her    scattered body


father sleepwalks        through good times
reruns          opaled      bedroom      light
night voluptuous      announces        itself
on black cricket phone  glossed hips of his
guitar      boots polished for the gig    he
soaps his face      shaves the holes in his
story    careful not to awaken his opposite
eye    pardon the metronome          in my
chest I've always kept faithful  the time of
the song      you wrote

                              oath of tricksters

# OAK FALLS

[los tios]    [so impressed with the little house]    [cheap as
the apartment in Brownsville]    [bigger than the trailer in
Edinburgh]    [todo nuevecito]    [someone else's dream
foreclosed]    [for our pink possibility]    [we must really
be making it]    [street: Oak Falls]    [our own front
yard]    [can you believe it!]    [our own young tree]
[nothing special for no one special]    [papery white
trunk]    [fan-shaped leaves]    [square-veined with a
velvety soft fuzz underneath]    [tender thing]    [anthills
formed at the tree's roots]    [Tio Javier drunk mowing]
[dumps poison onto the mounds]    [like chemo I guess]
[and after]    [the hurricanes blow in the bills]    [blow
by blow]    [mortgage rises with every flood]    [repo]
[lotto ticket drawerbursts]    [the water's oilslick ARM]
[chokehold]    [repo]    [  mold knocks out the house's
teeth  ]  [storms    [in the shape
[of names    [in anger                    [punch holes [ ]
into the wall ]    [ ]    [ ceiling sags with
                        mold                    ]
            [    ]    [pipes ever backing up]

[and I am asked to be obedient]    [can't use that
bathroom anymore]    [or this sink]    [stuck disposal]

[stove and fridge all we need]     [   ]      [the tree's loom
now branchbare]     [r ott  ed ou t]      [its corpse stays in
the ground]     [     FINAL NOTICE      ]      [every other
month]

                    [each new tree we try to plant]     [dies
too]     [     something wrong with the soil     ]

# DISSOCIATIVE STATES

1 It's February 16 Houston 1993 & the call from MD ANDERSON is a guillotine ring 2 each word Papi says si, ándale pues, si aqui está, & so he has to break the news the experimental treatment has failed 3 SE MURIÓ 4 [                    ] 5 I can't piece together any memory after except 6 when Mami & Tio Javier sat overwhelmed & silent, reddened faces among stacks of paper smoking at the table 7 trying to figure out how they will burn our Mamá 8 each taking turns with the phone 9 & at this point the story is a skip in the record 10 & I must ask you, reader for just one moment——

11 & we are in pain because our umbilical cords have grown back & root themselves to objects of vice 12 but mine is a braid snaking out of myself 13 to find its root in the pines 14 so when Mami begins to float above us & above the arroz boiling in floodwater & above the half-blue tv 15 & above Tio Javier drinking himself to death 16 & above her empty bed ever-missing my father 17 & thousands of crushed cigarettes 18 that tender umbilical cordon attaches itself to the rotting foreclosure so that she might not drift away but

18 every solid thing becomes itself backward 19 & we crane our necks to try & see where we are going 20 & we must have left something behind 21 what was backward is now forward & the trees press their thrashing branches into the glass & break in & drag me out by the hair 22 & the floodwater boils over onto the stove top 23 & a blue crab crawls out of the pot

24 I call to someone, try to warn, but I am suspended tighter still 25 my hair tangled up in leafy branches, toenails twisted into roots—

II.

26 & the drawers in the room open themselves 27 & floral skirts unfold themselves 28 & a pair of chestnut castanets tie themselves with curry-colored yarn 29 & together they find your form 30 & it's like you are here 31 are you here? 32 & the pibil & bitter orange & fabuloso faint on the air 33 & a fork pierces the yolk and the room swells with sun & someone 34 is here next to me & I am not alone 35 at the table after school boiling ramen I dance with floating plates 36 to José José 37 who I don't even like but I'm only ten and couldn't see how 38 cancered & in pain 39 the chestnut hairs felled silent from your head 40 placed themselves like saffron 41 into a pot of rice——

III.

42     *The archaeology of memory is like this:*

43     *a column of drawers hollowing their artifacts*

44     *your threadboned ribs*

45     *form the cathedral in which I kneel*

46     *to mourn the violences that devastated the soaring holiness*

47     *of your body & I repent*

48     *por mi culpa por mi culpa por mi gran culpa*

48     *I watch the cardinals we fed that day*

50     *knock their flight inside the sunspilled vault*


Fin     *& this is how I can go on, knowing you have returned home*

# GIRLBODY GIFT

first dress as a boy / an earlied eleven / iron papi's khakis
a dickies crease with white t-shirt / gel-comb black
slickback como linda / me and my girls look hard / get
caught / papi's hands crush my neck / *si no te compones* /
*te voy a matar* / *aquí no quiero jotas* // first kiss twelved /
chauncey saturnine centaur / trembling to jodeci // first
boyfriend tyrone mj smile / you want to go with me / spiral
perm and boyz II men II / sleep in his rockets jersey /
papi's backhand / *no quiero que andes con los pinches negros*
// first against / light-eyes cedric / dream prince of pines
/ appears at sleepover / the moon is a pill in my can /
dazed I kneel / dick a dark poppy / no a muffled petal in
my throat / not all my yet / tells his boys // first white
boy / summer night a stolen sapphire / justin shooting
stars on slide / three am taut orchid drum / mami
pregnant due to work at seven / searching the milky fog /
caught in her chevy's headlights / get the belt / *slut* to his
boys // bi furcate my head / shave bottom half / rocks
pelt my back on track / get the belt / *faggot dyke freak* /
and with all my new names / I can now fathom my father
/ his father / saying all the things he doesn't want me to
be // hospital roommate nicole / lily-firm breasts on

sterile white sheets / hillary pink vodka mattress / leigh

on tina and a yearning of triangles // seventeen / doctor

writes hymen intact // a knot hot and sharp as woodsalt /

on the chord in my starheart

# ASSIMILATION ROOMS

el día que nos fuimos de brownsville las tías nos dieron una bolsa de naranjas y sodas y unos paquetitos de tortillas calientitas hechas a mano con carne para el camino y en el u-haul papi nos manejó hasta hou-stón y cuando llegamos mami me compró ropita nueva para estrenar en el kinder y cada mañana abuelita me peinaba diferente a veces con bolas o una diadema y me dormía en su cuartito porque juntas veíamos novelas y rezábamos hincadas en frente de la virgencita y las velas y aunque casi no me podía comunicar en inglés en la escuela sí me encantaban los libros y no me molestaba estar solita sin embargo mi abuelita se puso malita de su cáncer y se tuvo que quedar en el hospital y mientras me iba a **the honey tree** después de la escuela con tanto miedo porque no entendía nada y los niños me gritaban cosas en inglés que hacia mal aunque no sabía nada de su mundo pero me dijo mi mamá que me portara bien entonces me callé y solo les dije a las maestras **I can read** porque quería estar sola **alone in this room** y los niños se burlaban que allí estaba **with the boogey man**[1] y me atrancaron la puerta y solo escribo esto para rogarte que por favor ábreme la puerta porque tengo mucho miedo y esta oscuro y todavía estoy aquí adentro con él

---

[1] The day we left from Brownsville the aunts gave to us a bag of oranges and sodas and little packets of warm tortillas made by hand with meat for the road and in the u-haul papi drive us all the way to hou-ston and when we got there mami buy me new little clothes for kinder and each morning grandma combing my hair different sometimes with balls or a headband and I sleep in her little room because together we can watching novelas and kneeling to pray to the virgin and the candles and though I could not barely communicate in English at school I did loved books and it not bother me to be little alone however my grandma got sick of cancer and stayed in the hospital and so I was tooken to the honey tree daycare after school but I was with so much fear because I did not understood anything and the kids scream at me things in English that making me feel bad even though I didn't know anything about their world but my mami told me to be good so I stop talking and just told the teachers I can read because I want I was alone by myself in this room and the children make fun that I was in there with the boogey man and so they lock the door lock me in and I just write this to beg to you please open me the door because I am very scared and is dark and I am still in here with him

as a choir girl    I was prohibited from
singing the songs I knew    in the piano
room    another kind of amor prohibido
*I get so weak in the knees    I can hardly speak*
no    that's vulgar singing    trained
singers  hold the note aloft    faithful so
pleasing to protestants    so taught out of
myself    I sing edelweiss    frère jacques
stille nacht   line up for oktoberfest    in a
theater    a bank    and C lunch    stuff
my tamed boca   with vinegar    bratwurst
& the finest  european feathers [2]

[2]"… in the environments that adopt assimilation policies and devalue children's culture of origin, schools and parents may feel pressured to assimilate children into mainstream culture for children's survival and success, resulting in further loss of culture of origin and/or marginalization from both cultures." —Yoon, Eunju, et. al. "Content Analysis of Acculturation Research in Counseling and Counseling Psychology: A 22-Year Review." *Journal of Counseling Psychology*, Vol. 58, No. 1 (January 2011): 83-96.

in gym admire   whitegirl nipples      soft & pink
as sow's ears       so unlike your own dark      in
physics learn *parallax*:      the effect of position
upon viewing an object       in english learn the
greats are from europe new york      use *parallax* in
a poem      b minus      learn your place      is
beneath[3]      the blondes who snitch      on you
see them off to college      from behind a register
a farewell to arms      on the road      they're bound
for   europe harvard   columbia new york   cash
your check      at the veteran's memorial quikcash
know your place   is going nowhere   wrong side
of the highway      crime forest they call us      in
government      argue with mr. lockwood      who
teaches the confederate flag      means *state's rights*
DETENTION before work      apron stinks up your
backpack      catch a ride      learn to serve
classmates with a smile      at home   help mami
lavar los baños      to even get to go      to the
dollar theater   even after popcorn      your hands
still smell raw       from the comet and bleach
2am feed the baby      so mami can sleep      shave
your fingers & toes      before school      scrub the
dark off your nipples      in gym clock      a seven
minute mile   clean cotton morning      the only
ahead you get      parallax:   the effect of position
upon viewing an object[4]

---

[3] *Patient trauma      death maternal   primary caretaker   failure to acculturate in childhood      late english acquisition   depressive   oppositional defiant   school predominantly culturally American   home environment predominantly of the heritage culture      working class   abuse*

[4] "This association is purported to reflect, in part, the impact of negative experiences faced by immigrants in the process of assimilation, i.e. acculturative stressors. However, these findings can be explained by high levels of risk for psychiatric disorder among the US-born members of ethnic minority populations, who have both high risk for psychiatric disorders and high levels of acculturation relative to immigrants."— Breslau, Joshua, et. al. "Migration from Mexico to the US and Subsequent Risk for Depressive and Anxiety Disorders: A Cross-National Study." *Arch Gen Psychiatry*. 2 011 April; 68(4): 428–433.

1995   budding black    swallow each received
blue  eye        that  watches        your  house
tongued    in their language   after midnight
whitewash every brown    bikini thrill    cut
& sell     that wild black braid:    america's
cash       pawn used blue eyes      on your
peroxide tongue   take out your original eyes
& replace       pull  your  people's  melodies
lamenting doves   out of your ears    plug the
wound  with  hot           and  thick forgetting
nevermind    your mysterious origin      each
milk tooth   a little bloodrot   in virgin linen
each plait of river    in your head     unravels
your  brightening  body           from  corpus
(luckily so luckily here)    each day a passing
(cross leg uncross)   new record          hidden
track:    nevermind    nameless  overwritten

"This association is purported to reflect, in part, the impact of negative experiences faced by immigrants in the process of assimilation, i.e. acculturative stressors. However, these findings can be explained by high levels of risk for psychiatric disorder among the US-born members of ethnic minority populations, who have both high risk for psychiatric disorders and high levels of acculturation relative to immigrants." — Breslau, Joshua, et al. "Migration from Mexico to the US and Subsequent Risk for Depressive and Anxiety Disorders: A Cross-National Study."

*Arch Gen Psychiatry.* 2011 April ; 68(4): 428–433.

INCIDENT: Nothing             an immigrant's
daughter does       is intelligible.      We were
lenient      on her      you understand:      the
boys well        they have promise.           Pity.
Bright girl.      Girls with   HONOR     don't have
these        kinds of problems. Zero tolerance.
We'll show that     involuntary body.   Its spill
from contours.      That    language       has no
place    in this class

                                    break that       dark horse
still bucking       a tighter bridle    don't believe
you        young lady       stealing       or giving it
away      like that      EXPEL            truck driver
border filth      they have no place       in this
palimpsest          CUFFS WHILE WE              LOOK
THROUGH YOUR
nothing an
        immigrant's daughter does    is defensible


first-generation          don't make it the last
you can be anything   in America    especially
when you're made        an example


PUNISHMENT: ONE   STRIKE.           Or, petrified
lightning.   A storm's release      drowned wild
in white sand;           a heat          assimilated
ever-rooting    its permanent ·

                                              shatter[5]

[5] Gómez, Francisco C., Ronn Johnson, Qiana Davis, Roberto J. Velásquez. "MMPI—A Performance of African and Mexican American Adolescent First-Time Offenders." August 1, 2000. *Psychological Reports*, Vol 87, Issue 1, pp. 309 – 314.

# ASSIMILATION PROGRESS REPORT

GYM     learn whitegirl nipples     are your     erotic shame     the only body
you long for     is hers     shotgun pass the smoke     in the locker room
shower     run for hours     even when they throw rocks     at your head
because they found out     you're a dyke

PHYSICS learn     1. *parallax, (n.)* the effect whereby an object appears to differ
according to viewer position     2. *matter (n.)* physical substance which
occupies space; an affair or situation under consideration; the reason for
distress or a problem:     3. the tricks of English     tricks of the trade

TEXAS HISTORY     learn a swindle:     Mexico lost     its pacific goldveined
mountains     to someone else's destiny     manifest     MULTIPLE CHOICE
a. be quiet     b. as paperwork     so that the cotillion     may accept
their blond praise     their every award     c. hold hands with their whiteboy
d. raise your question     e. they'll escort you out     put you in BASIC
with     the Other     f. not HONORS material

ENGLISH     *On the Road*     white boys' aching oats     are high literature     high
and well-funded wandering     while papi     is pulled over     in that same
desert     asked to show his papers     before el baile     learn Sal Paradise
loved a Mexican girl     but not enough     to name her     and shh
Brandon from Wimbledon     is talking     and he is three-story brilliant
ha ha ha     the voices     that *matter (n.)*     are the people     who *matter (n.*
ivybright and ivory

GOVERNMENT     learn     confederate flag     is *state's rights*:     on the test that
doublespeak     that makes right a boundless estate     makes rightless     th
bound black body     confederate flag stickers     on mudspun jee
puka shelled     the boys go ridin     protected as a plantation     the *founder*
holy signatures     guarantee it, you see     a. their liberty     b. our terro

WORK     learn     to wipe that (with a) smile     off your face     from three p.m
to one a.m.     sidework then homework     use the front computer
to clock in and out     otherwise in the back room     his hand     will har
between my legs again     the booths empty     after midnight

EXPULSION     lighter confiscated     alternative school     at morning patdown
turn out pockets     white tongues     snitch     bag check     arms u
someone's head slammed     on cement bricks     1. *parallax,* (n.) the effect o
position     upon viewing an object

SIGNATURE: _____

# GULF PINES, or FINAL ASSIMILATION ROOM

*after Frida Kahlo's Wounded Deer*

PATIENT STATES: honeysuckle wraps        its heated
bruise    of bad news—      a daughter bound by
trouble    is a wilder grief    manifested bodily
oilthick stars        pour down their      vines to
overwhelm    the moldsprung house    stormwater
sags the walls        as the ghost spine blossoms
berries of rot    in her daughter's daughter's brains
the girl doubledbled      shares a heart with the
pines      pulls the vein from the blade      antlered
illness          made creature        punished into
deformity    suspended mid-run        an animal
body's instinct      is to survive pain      and flee its
hunter        the girl attached to the      thrashing
creature        is calm, nearly smiling        another
another another      of us   in a hospital room[6]

---

[6] "When you talk to the parents of these juvenile offenders, you get the same old story: "Johnny stayed out late, he was moody, he skipped school ... but, we figured he'd grow out of it." They don't. Recently, I found out about a family-oriented adolescent treatment program that's getting through to these kids—and it's often covered by health insurance. If you have a troubled teenager, don't wait until he gets here, get help now." Television commercial for HCA Gulf Pines Psychiatric Hospital. The speaker is an older white male judge putting on his robe in his quarters, surrounded by leather bound books.

GULF PINES PSYCHIATRIC HOSPITAL PATIENT INTAKE PHOTO, 1996.

# THE SIRENS

Mamá floats
　　　paper prayers

　　　into trees:
this is the language
　　　she speaks to the missing
a siren of boys
　　　encircle the house
*Who has led our daughter astray?*
boys blink blue

　　　*Just another brown*
　　　　　*girl lost*
*like the rest*

# TROPICAL DEPRESSION

The storm is a sustained chord: from the eye of the hurricane

the belt lashes swing out     for talking back

the rain a gathered salt   and blood   hair shed—


To begin this story     view us as god does:   a gulf

swept white   a darkened sound   or, women muted by water,


                I inherit a palace of locked doors.


          My father parks   broken down cars        in my chest

    mother in a Chevy Beretta   running vulgar     as a garbage disposal

       and so I learn:    trouble is lonelier.

The storm stretches its legs   in this city   the ocean is always knocking

    on your door

       slicktongued and thick with oil and ants

and the pines too   long to be underwater

    with the rest of us—

Up the block Marcel and them do thundering layups

beneath a quilt of black clouds

while my father teases out     a George Benson tune     alone on his guitar

to an audience     of the news


tonight I am an overheated moon     pulling at the waters,

the grandest river     casts a silk egg     into the pear-shaped gulf—

I make warriors of the ocean,

to obliterate borders, explode walls, overwhelm the fences     uncross the river


For the great violences hidden inside women

For the women hidden inside great violences;

# THIRTEEN

Scan the leaves on the dress, the cardinal in flight. Recuerdalo: oiled lion, tubed to the nose. Pardon the line of ripped bread on dried wood, the yield of red ranunculus and peony ruffled. Parallel lines keep the wolf circling, our heads snarled. It says so in the cards. A charge in the blood. A crimson muscle twisted in ink. A pool of rotting oranges. Twin girls joined at the nape. A record spinning in a fog-draped living room, violins gathered in bouquets. To resuscitate. A shatter of rain before the world drains into the gulf. Tilt the tin bowl toward the mouth. Round the dogs in the clearing, bind their claws with hair. Respetame. I was thirteen when I first felt a blonde boy. I still cough up his cornsilk, wind the spit in my fingers. Fresh white breasts in the grass. Brown nipples like mushrooms. July rubied with red stars. Boys float their bicycles into the trees. No one gets in trouble but us. Blackberries erupt over the river. We escape a patrolling moon. Trespassing is passage. Is there a plan to dip the girl in ink, to lustre the hook from which she will droop. The jaw hangs open. The yard is lousy with dead dogs. To resuscitate. To resuscitate.

# CARDINALS, A NOVENA

above the pines
      a glass apple

put a thought
      inside it

for example  [ *red* ]


      [ bordertown station wagon   filled with
          my infant selves     sinks         into rio bravo ]


            [ the cardinals dive lured by
                torn       hard bread ]


[ *Angelica* hairs unweave
      our cancered head ]


      [ childwhite panties      made mother-ready   the day
              that purpled clot   in her spine   begins its kill ]


[ guadalupe   jeweled virgin    wax glass   candle
      entre todas las mujeres   we kneel to push away the final night ]


[ get well heart balloons lose hope   sink in the hospital room   as morphine
      bladders rise   tias asleep   too ascending toward a february dawn ]

[ we children    touch our wet    honeysuckle kudzu
      lay on old tires    our lips ache that bayou gulf steam ]

[ cherries in the snow, first
              lipstick I ever stole ]

[ *faggot slut* spray-painted    on driveway
           flat and plain  as  ]

The end:

I run through a knot of shifting trees
      toward an empty ballad that plays on loop

          song without source
              *amor eterno*    *inolvidable*

    a muffled sun
      split by pines

*rib one*      *shoulder two*      *hip three rib*    *five*    *shoulder*    *spine six*
  *neck*  *breast*    *womb nine*

to join a line-
    age of burdened beasts

gashes that bloom cardinals
    swooping in and out             of my brains

[

passing

  ]

]

hemmed

]

 [

silvered

]

 [

tooth

]

[

unspooled

]

[

work

  ]

[

passing

]

 [

ululate

]

   :

impenetrable

   :

    :

cervix

   :

    :

vase

    :

   :

hollowbody

   :

   :

cho
rd

    :

afford

   :

slapped

   :

lily

    :

tumor

   :

glass

]

petal

]

[

morphine

 ]

[

grafted

  ]

[

suspended

]

wristbound

 ]

[urge

thinning

 ]

bud

]

 [

breast

]

[

belly

# A HALO OF BEASTS

an ancestral bestiary

# PRAYING HERD: FOR SAFE JOURNEY

Draw a line through our scattered bodies. The pattern of fallen calves in this meadow will mirror the constellation above. Look up. We whip our tails to a silent song:

We sing to the moon, ask for wings to lift our flock to heaven;
We plead to the moon, since she will take pity;
We beg of the moon since she changes, as our circumstance must also change;
We repent to the moon to release the dead in her unspooling;
We praise the moon who gives birth to herself;
We venerate the moon our scarred mother;
We confess to the moon since she is forlorn, as we are forlorn;
We call to the moon since she passes, as we must also pass;
We pray to the moon since the forest is her echo, and we are made in her visage;
We sing to the moon, ever-abandoned by the sun, as we are also abandoned

# HORNED WOMAN ANCESTOR

pig hearts on table
good salted beast

    splayed amidst bursts of
    petals and our naked feet

at noon we birth
that clement knot

    little fists of bloodhair
    emerge sacred from the mound

    and she arrives

beneath the forest floor
the earth opens & yawns

    brassbright fish
    bursts of fragrant red fruit

and after the atrocity
my daughters will walk

    along the palm of God's hand
    to find me——

I will know you by your heavy horns and two faces
to look always South as you look North

to survive this nightmare so American
where you count coins

you do not have

# CARMEN, ANCIENT BASS

You only knew my body wrinkled as oak bark eroded by
water, greying with a slow life that has not been

kind to me, except for its sparing; my whip, my shimmer,
my morena agile so long and copper lush this beauty

common, forgotten, but when you my children
come, peaches fall into my rivers, their flowers crown

your rareness emerging from that primal place I hid
your tender, bright egg, my many children, the river

is too fast in your blood and on this our cut
land and these my thin-tissued fins, they are for

cradling nietos y bisnietos so helpless but for
their fight upstream away from that silted salt tomb

and so for you, I escape from the ranchos,
protect you from the hurters whose names will drown

in your triumph and if I catch fifty stars in my
mouth for each of you I will grow arms to embrace

each life sprung from me, learn to walk on land
and miracle these failing organs to bright fruits

for you, ay hija, hijo, como me duele dejarte
but at the end of this life, I drift into the current

knowing you will be heroes

# GUADALUPE, STAR-HORNED TAURUS

That I commune with the dead as I oil your feet. My house at the throat of the river, the door to this world, I wait for you. That I ask of the spirit and receive the knowledges: yerbabuena, vela de virgen, baño de alhucema. Cut the joint at the hoof & fatten the soup. Accept this offering, thank the plant. That I love you with the knowledge of our ways lost to violence. That you will call me up from the silt in your bones.

On my final night on this earth, the smoke pours from my nostrils. I cut the cards. The melon in the moon, the rose climbing a ladder. Thick coins in my cup. That my heart closes its fist. That my body succumbs to its constant nurture.

What you will say in my memory: that my serenity. That my softness. That my skirt is the sky pattern. That the cedars kneel for my passage. That my laugh was kind. That your feet carry my body. That I am the helix the roses climb. That the illness spreads north as we cross. That these are the end days. That heaven groans blood. That I have scienced the stones into a circle. That they speak of failure. My daughters.

Agony in the garden.

# CARLOS, WOUNDED COYOTE

Feathers crowd my sharp mouth with unbearable softness, coat my tongue with everything baby-fine. Laughter and laughter. My rough play. My black nails. My sunswept broad. I expert meat from the wilderness for mine, my pack, my riverwed brilliances.

Asi, mijito: discard the beak & the wattle, the tumored skin hanging from the chicken head. Cell-splitting disease. This stone in my belly, this sugared gash in my foot, it grounds my body. I am confused by this dream, my back to the earth & the dying laughter. Each mother gone is a plank gouged from my liver. The cluster of knots in my kidneys. The dying laughter. I push my face against yours, and yours.

Orange moon rolls over the old coast in heaven's lace.

*What I did: I carried each of them.*

Vallarta, I return. Rest.

# O, CASADA

& what night will reveal you / your shifting camouflage / your every plausible story / I too end up wedded to / the apologue of my mothers: / mountain panther / undetectable / you hunt from aloft / & in all your enigmatic unseen / all I can do is resign / to sleep singing / in the clean canyons / I have cleaned / await until I wake alone // the stranger children who too much resemble you / my inarticulate love / lately all I remember / of your face / is the back of your head / as you walk away / I lay next to / a body of absence / so untouched I am / again a new bride / and so I make and make a home for you / I raise and raise the sun for you / learn to listen to the women / in my bones / who have already survived you / & don't you know it dear / you are not so imperceptible / I see it all now / with my body / a knowing so inherited / I am pregnant with eyes

# ESCAPE, A WAXWING MIGRATION

On either side, the land is white-clean.

Hunger and hunger, my young love steals me away. Like every mother before me. Far berry fields, tangerine flower stars, thick chard, jewels of cabbage. Migrate the meridian, sift powdery sand for fruitrot. My back bent for picking, my belly grows. Nesting is work is nesting.

When I was good, I was an apple blush on brown, my father's pride. He, mine.

Father, lover, a truck, and each caught homemade bruise. A truck, a lover made father and here I am again, a beetroot knot on my face, my hands bound by sharp grasses, once pearled strands of sunlight, plenty in their bending.

The men who love you have a backhand for every desire. Wild carrot, potato, corn. Strange cold lands.

The eggs hatch, stranded from home.

# BESTIA

little whip      study the map            in the moon take
this pink comb      a lighter    and this limp-spined
wallet    mira      I put this      paper in it:      THESE
ARE THE INSTINCTS      YOU WILL NEED          TO CROSS
stay in the light        do not wait          for anyone
except for the        little one      these are the phone
numbers      do not make friends        these are the
safe houses        & the women who      will repair
your shoes      nice men are never nice      when they
are starving        if they ask you        who is waiting
en el otro lado        for you        tell them no one
that every step      is a prayer        for the impossible
pay the coyote        this amount        put the rest asi
in your panties          put it even          where love
cannot cross        but mija      you are loved      our
prayers      will protect you      this land          has
always belonged        to you      don't cry      don't be
afraid      don't cry      don't be afraid        don't cry
don't be afraid        no llores        no tengas miedo

# AURELIO, SEER TECOLOTE

The sky is veined with light from an imploded star, a dense magic threaded with blood.

O Madre, let their walk into the desert not undo their life;
O Madre, to the North there are whips of light in the sky & a ship of welded stars, an immensity of bodies;
O Madre, to the Northwest a hanged man swings between cliffs, his feet batter the canyon, trees bend in pale wailing;
O Madre, to the West the sun has extinguished forever, & the demon sits on the lid of the world & prevents the sunrise with his coded babbling;
O Madre, to the Southwest the bodies are purpling midstride in the dust, wedded to this weakened hour;
O Madre, to the South the gate is flooding, the water approaches black & swollen, faces emerge in the rushing;
O Madre, to the Southeast the mossbearded trees are dusted white & graves are churning;
O Madre, to the East the houses blow apart like paper, horses tumble in the wind;
O Madre, to the Northeast the fairy sea captures children in its lightning, demonhair fraying the sky;

I turn my head with open eyes, and cannot stop its turning.

# RAM, LABORER

*for my mother*

When I came to the US, I never had iced tea. It's not that good. Pero I love Coca Cola. & I am obsessed with hamburgers! Me encanta este país, its music. That we can make it on our own. As long as you work hard. It's why I waitress all night and work cashregister in the day. No diploma pero no importa, I walk fast and stand tall in my work. I coax flowers into stories. Still, I dance. I do this all para mi mamá, mi abuelita, mi hermano. For all of our second chances. We escaped him. And him. I will never throw that away. I only use Revlon. It's the best. You see this eyeshadow? *Wintercloud.*

Mi esposo is the best guitarist in the valley and he says I am his song in the distance and he is also my song in the distance. Our little trailer in the sand. When our baby girl is born I will give her any life she wants, dress her in new clothes, buy her a little house, name her a name you can only say in English so that she will be American and because it is the language of all the beautiful and cruel things.

# BETO, SHEEP OF HEAVEN

*for my father*

you stand in the field    a thin grace

booted & bell bottomed

la zona rosa    Reynosa nights    just a little distorted

maybe you will have made it    in America by now

sixth grade dropout    does not contain that genius


felt-edged notebooks    their precise light pencil    on the staff

just a fourteen year-old boy    on a bus alone

to Mexico City    ready to ignite the stage    les paul    warm

cream    wail    afro just so    magazine spread ready

what crossing would not nurture    such a rareness


but this side would rather    break its own mountains


                than let you——

they call you

        too foreign


too sentimental    too delicate    too complex


each word    a blade    to your softness


        a shot    a wound in your head so


    the stars pour out


drain their light into the gulf

        drown your music

it's not your fault

we have always       run toward the wrong
                  lights

a glow so ecstatic               as it is in your dream

# JAVIER, LOST JAGUAR

O bruise of Christ, O flowering scar, bless
this station & let my truck barrel through
the night, so dense with lust

so that the honey bourboned stack of
coins in my mouth will open the world
cloaked between shifts of hard dark    my
scrap eighteen wheeler    dream    drum
charging    the road dotted with stars
   no love found    in the headlights

a lion's mane warms the sky    I    entomb
this dense calm in you O mother, drive
into the throat of the plainfields    rags
of raw grass    mourning you

# TO HIDE A GODDESS

*for Juan Diego and the Virgen of Guadalupe*

Crescent moon with eight-pointed star, she is the ornament strung taut in barren winter branches. Her voice is a moonbeam caught wild in a white throat. I climb this mound of ruins to beg her back to us, the disappearing.

Robed in roses, hunterbride, seven flowered snake, unmad this land from grief. Emerge from the soil as you emerge from the light. They bruise our heads, they bruise our heads, knife in new language. Winged star, descend onto this flank of night, this pearled nightmare. Lost, so many children. I am a father to my loneliness.

*After nightfall, follow the old path toward windy peaks. Look to the cloud womb. I will dazzle you with bright blood, red as spring roses. Gather the blooms in your tilma. Present yourself to the white Christ, a murder shrouded. I weave for us a shield of fire. Read instead my painted prayers. I am here, I who am your mother.*

# WHO WAITS AT THE LAKE

In the loam
    I am pulled
    blood to salt

        longing to water——

leaves hang midair
    turn strange magic

surround the lake
    a column

walk through the curtain
    of floating leaves and look

        upon water steel——

watch of animals
    at the rim

turned to stone
    eyes hollowed

limbs
    weeping ossified

terror
    or grace

hazard my body
    seeking you

    still

still

and this is the trick:

the act of waiting
    the nature of stone

# ORÁCULO

(you miraculous body)    (comet entombed in water)    (what tissue)    (has unraveled)

(this forest)    (in you)    (rot thought)    (slow bewildered bone)    (your burden spine)

(taught to cower)      (you work)      (you worry)      (your womb gathers)    (names from)

(the milkwhite river)    (inky shadowland)    (of the original people)      (still lives in you)

(its wooded heart)      (in emergency)      (you carry)      (its story:)

(this forest)      (is a condition)      (of exile)      (your descent from)      (it iterates)

(like this:)        (wound)      (womb)      (wound)      (womb)

(possible outcome:)

(your body)      (the bridge)      (your body)    (pulled apart)      (your body)

(itself)        (the crossing)      (our feet)      (making passage)      (upon your back)

# MALINALLI

history is a woman slandered     say I am
traitor     but forget I am     the grass     a
daughter     of the old people     listen:  an
orphan     I was sold     chained to the
ocean     his beard     his breath     on my
bound     body made to take     and take
the milkwhite river     into my womb     my
doubling tongue     serves the ship     to live
and so this illness     begins of a violation
this country begins     of a violation  in the
dark     between seas     in the palace of ribs
begun in me     and so     my daughters
inside the monster     cribbing our young
in its teeth     through liver     & spine     &
sinew     I bride the rivers     across time
& find our people     & steal back our
riches     hide among deer     disappear into
the forest     where reunited     we will spill
& spill & spill     spread like a flood

# GLASS TRAIL

sometimes     a     clear
night    sometimes miles
lost   the lightning roots
down      & needles the
earth           & the trail
smokes          & a lens
forms  in  the  ground
we peer down       & in
a confusion of glass &
verify     the     journey
commit  our  sinew  to
that length   vined with
minnows         bruised
mica       a stream of
water      unspools our
blood  into  ruby  stars
turning in the diamond
cold      & in that river
rush we lose half of us
the   milky   way   of
minnows  connects  to
the   river  taking   its
bodies  that  sail  limp
toward shaggy pines

# SEA OF DROWNED CALVES

The dunes whip up into hives. The bladed saltgrasses braid to the memory of water, ache toward the tide. We drag ourselves through beach pews, through the scene of axed water, of spoiled sea. Moon howls raw over silvered sand, the foamed water a tilted gloss. The incense of brine, the rotated stars, the powdered quartz. Tongues of water attempt toward the pack. Ill waves crave new skulls to grind. Each snowy surf blossoms polished vertebrae, fractioned horns. In the water, floating hands. Fishes dart in and out of mouths. A calf washes up limp, broken from the ruffled surge. Then another. Another. A music of corpses on the coast. A stun in each pair of wide brown eyes. A bawl from the herd, a surge of thunder.

The cycle of tides implies circles, as if beginning ever met end, recognized it.

# THE STRANDED LAMB

1 It was told that at the top of the mountain, one could find the stranded lamb surrounded by a dome of floating moths. 2 After the boats arrived, the purification, the brushfires, the chaos of locusts, the wars on the pyrite cliffs, & the opening of field, the lamb climbed the mystic ladder up the mountain & would not descend. 3 The cursed seek the lamb to feed it & bring it water in oblation. When they find it, it is unwell. 4 Pustules dot its eyes & sludge its lashes; its body withers in starvation & thirst; its fleece clots with flies. Maggots soft & white as rice bloom from its belly; its brown fleece blows away in the frigid air. 5 It bends its head & offers its body. It is already dead. 6 To seek the lamb is to starve; do not eat from its flesh, but suffer as it has suffered. 7 To suffer is to comprehend history. 8 To gaze upon suffering is to shatter the heart & devastate the mind. 9 To see betrayal. 10 Who crushes them with this tempest, & bitters the night? 11 The earth belongs to the wicked: the ocean blackens, the earth balds, sky churns to blood. 12 & the animals mourn. The lamb cannot follow, & so they l eave it, unsaved in the wilderness.

# UNSPOOLED TIDE

In fire, we discover our human parts: hooves split into toes then fuse again, hair unravels from buffalo heads, bristled fur recedes, regrows in the dark. We scarcely remember our flesh forms, or recognize our ownership.

To find the original light is to find the source body. In albedo, we ache toward the firs. We run toward utter dark.

The water wall topples over, crashing down on us in long, foamy loops, as if it were hair tumbling down the canyon's great white shoulders.

# BORDER SEMIOTICS

Rags of clotted blood on bone on Walmart tee-shirt threaded with work on raw hand & wood brained in silver bloody tooth cloth missing chancla a packed truck toward the destiny star to enter the gold pear night, ghosts in an elk eye, land of cold evenings

Illegal

Pal norte guey pa gozar pa comprar botas y trocas y casas pa mi vieja pa mis hijos pa mi mamá pa mi papá porque me da la chingada gana porque me lo merezco orale a jalar con ganas mijito mijita

Dreamer

Milk north milk honey milk mall milk truck milk maid milk child milk milked fuck milk

Promised Land

Anchor baby beaner cheech cholo chuco clown car coyote dirty sanchez fence hopper gordita greaser illegal jumping bean manuel labor mexcrement pachuco pool-digger roach spic tire-hugger vato wetback

Freedom of Speech

Day of the Dead edition Starbucks Mexican Shade Grown Organic Fair Trade coffee with Mexican hot chocolate and cinnamon jalapeño, free saint bracelet included, Virgen de Guadalupe tattoo

Free trade manifest destiny market market market

Tattered corpse disintegrates on XY axis flesh ripens purple a flush rot & tongue a plain of flies if you drown in the river blessed are the meek

Invisible

# A FIELD OF ONIONS: BROWN STUDY

*dedicated to the immigrants buried in mass graves in and near Falfurrias, Texas*

1. I walk through a bald field blooming violet onions. I will know I am absolved when there is no more dirt underfoot, when I have flipped the earth and the river runs above us, a glassed belldark sound.

2. To find: liver, lung, womb. A lens cut from vulture eye. This is what it is to miss a thing.

3. At the McDonald's, a man in a parked car will talk himself awake. This is another kind of hunger.

4. A prayer for the king: forty pears, all bloomed from young throats. Long life, a sea of rice, a thicket of braids.

5. Problem: Four boats arranged in a cross drift away from each other in opposing directions. What theory states that, all conditions remaining equal, they can reach each other again on the other side of a perfect globe?

6. To understand a map is to shrink the world; to plan; to color.

7. Can you smell the vinegar blood in the babes, stardappled. The survivors ride the beast train toward the North, over those rolled off onto the tracks. See their legs, scattered.

8. Olga in Minnesota: to be with her mother amidst rags of spring snow. For now, she is curled in the glovebox of a Chevrolet Cavalier.

9. Bless you, all that meat and milk, threaded. Pass, you fairer animal. Not you. I have seen the door in the water.

10. Solution: Magical thinking.

11. To panic is to feel all your wildness at once.

12. A flock of geese felled to the open plain, the lush grass confounds even the birds for passable angles.

13. We the holy, are never really still. Agitation pulls even at hanging planets.

14. Four sirens twist their voices—four dead in the desert borderlands.

15. In this dream, I am on a plane. I wake up to the pilot smiling down on me. No one flies the plane. Or, I am flying the plane.

16. The threads fly loose on each body, some sown to others, some not. But let's not take this metaphor too far; we are better than the obvious.

17. A hero is a plane of being.

18. I think of a girl at space camp, perched above a better telescope than she has in her room. Tonight, she figures space as a map of horses. Blur, focus. Blur and focus. Tonight, the clouds will pull apart for her. Tonight, we will all dream of horses.

19. My ancestor says: *Later, when I arrive at your house, I will hang a crown of flowers at your door. And yours. And yours.*

20. And: *Sometimes I choose to come through your television. In sleep, you will mistake me for dripping water. You will think you heard your father. We visit each other in these ways.*

21. Plan B. From the moon, the earth is a crown of dark marble.

22. There are varying kinds of tragedy that produce the same outcome: paperwork.

23. And even if we did save the trees, or the whales, the hunger would still be so great the people who need saving would still need saving.

24. The heads of violet onions, rooted child fingers, blue-leafed lips. An orchard, a mass grave.

25. I give you my coat and scarf in offering. I have no choice, I was born to saints in pilgrimage.

26. Paper-purple skin. Grounded bodies. The border. A field of onions.

27. Thesis: I swallow a bee for each ill deed done. I am a hive walking. I strain to hear you over the regret.

# BEAST MERIDIAN

THE ANIMALS                          CROSS.

girl               never            torn into in your center—

forget this night sky          your body into halves

the widening line that splits     to home. In grief,

was always a star map         let your middle open

body and breast to earth,       hurt & this is your

toward that old strange        dream its starry dark

deep memory:                vined with heavy flowers

and long trees              you find your dead

the afterland where           at each animal constellated

gaze always upward            forming its language

in your inner knowing

*mictlan*                    *nepantla*

that which separates         you from home

you from history             you from your mothers

every star pattern             is a watchful grace

find their names  &  the split will heal  &  return the land

to that lineless open   join hands with   the invisible

the disappeared       the forgotten      river flooding

the land nourished    the blooming mourning

                                     the return of the beasts

# LOPEZ, PRAYING HERD: REQUIEM

Draw                     a line                    through

        our          scattered          bodies

    the meadow        reveals          our      constellation.

THE WAY BACK

It begins with the estrangement from the land, born into a system of dreaming, of dreaming about the dream. This dream divides the land into low dwellings and high. Where the uncursed live—north of somewhere. All beings born into the dream feel its old unhealable wound. To live, she journeys heavy with the leaving and at the end of the passage, she is bound to cruel work. To live, she must dip her hands into a pool of blood, then scrape it off with bleach. This land is a bewildering system of false signs. Misinterpreting those signs leads to punishment. Everyone knows how it works unless it works against them. One day, an uncursed boy invites her into the pines. He holds her hand. He commands the leaves to shiver like coins and suspend in the air. They float down to her. Because he has shown her himself, she will give him her human body. He brings down amethyst planets and feeds them to her, one by one. She drinks from a stream. I am not lost, she thinks, as years pass.

The uncursed are the corn-fed sons, inheritors of the kingdom, all sinew and muscle and good blond genes. The West has lain down for their conquest, they are told, and this boy is meant to go speeding toward a golden sun on Ben White Boulevard because darling had a future clear and white so plowed and so fertile so certain for a certain type of boy from a certain type of family, fashioned from wheat and sun and warm yellow days in warm yellow kitchens with a warm white mother humming in a room thick with flour and him in his bedroom eggshell blue with cows outside singing him Texas lullabies as he sleeps and wakes up a man with a promised destiny.

But before this triumphant conquest, he finds the girl, fashioned from dark clay and black mold and an ancient illness so sugared over so girled to sound, a wail spilled from womb to womb, each screaming mother another survival who, cropping her hair and furious, streaked the town with her sobbing, *Llorona*, and if not taken by violence, and not taken by grief, and not taken by illness, and not taken by poverty, and not taken by neglect, and not taken by cruelty, will sit in the woods like the women before her and devise her own end, savage and strange as birth.

And he made her believe he would choose her. This angered his family so white that his mother lined up all the blonde marriageable girls around the neighborhood and introduced him to each one as they clustered in the cul-de-sacs, tumbled from their windows, jumped off of trampolines, swam out of jeweled water pools, clamored out of lockers. The lines were so long that the girls worried about getting lost or left behind, so they braided their blonde hair together so that the cornsilk rope stretched and stretched and stretched to the end of his Texan kingdom, and they came, one by one, to his door.

According to legend, every mother in the white kingdom is given an elixir of white poppy to rub on her son's temples to forget and banish dark girls from his bed. The kingdom takes back the boy's coins, charges her interest. For failing to pay, she is labeled a criminal, made ever suspicious. It takes her possessions, her work, her livelihood, her family into its system of violence, debt, forgetting. And so, discarded by the dream, she finds herself stranded outside of it, stripped, forgotten. Her hands buckle and fist and her nails bind her fingers hard together into tough hooves. She walks through tangles alone into the pines, and there she is whipped by bare branches, where her skin welts and opens and her blood mixes with moonlit water. Where she eats raw fish crouched by the bank. Where she lets her sadness flow into the river.

The girl takes a knife to her scalp and crops her hair, braids the wild black strands to each branch as offering. She remembers her father's suffering, her mother's, her grandmother's, all of her family, mourning this similar way. Traveling to the top of the mountain, she begs to be made the moon, to lure all suns with her song into the darkness. Tries to believe in the dream. She runs through the forest in the old way, her grief becomes passage—into the land, into her body, into the waters of herself and all the mothers before her. Beneath the surface of the river she hears their voices, in the rustle of the trees she begins to know the world.

Cardinals swoop down from the trees to surround the girl. She has seen the ways of the kingdom, the way it sees her, the lie of the dream. And at the slightest expression of anger, she is detected, her animal form no longer passing in this new consciousness.

She is trapped in a state of night among the pines, a monstrous antlered creature wed to her grief. She canters through the woods, overcome with a loneliness that manifests as flowers that burst forth from her antlers. She runs East toward the dawn, but the clouds gather their ink in the sky. No one in the white kingdom can see the girl, or remember her.

In her exile, the girl has found a foamy river that crashes down the mountainside. It is a source of her new work, its weaving, capable of nurture or destruction. The treetops scrape the ceiling of stars, their predictable pattern. She watches them turn overhead, begins to recognize forms in the sky: the lion, the ram, the sheep, the coyote. The tragic beasts, trapped in their spinning. In this way, she counts away years of her life, her youth given up to survive the exile. The work of breaking the spell that has cast her into invisible darkness. She fashions a crown of constellations, links their stories into a halo. Her open, wild eyes grow clear with language. Her heart is a vibrating hum in her chest, a red dark wound beneath her glossed fur. To get out of the forest, she realizes, she must be the first to tell their story.

A river of planets, the bear, the ram, the scales, all the narratives of the West, the white kingdom. But as the years pass, the girl unspools animal after animal from her halo and writes its story into her sky so that the forgotten animals are revealed, the lines around the constellations redrawn so that she might pull up the dawn and break the impassable border between darkness and light, visibility and invisibility, high dwellings and low. Watch for her to burst forth, to command the dawn, to scream to life, victorious in her story.

Pearl of dawn in her window. A stream of animal bodies crosses the moat, thousands upon thousands breaching the edge of the dark. Stripped grey branches burst forth new flowers. Poppies unearth their nod. Grasses spindle through the parking lots, grasp the edges of billboards, strip malls, toppling their corners. The name of every violated body appears in the sky. The ocean glistens with the rising backs of the lost, those who have passed lifted in death toward home. The earth's bodies, each in their own way, recover the realm of the living to give to the dead of their origin, repair the seams between worlds along its meridians.

# ESTRELLADA

no distance I horizon might bewilder that

                     loneliness persisting its constant hunt—

an old companion, it silvers its way into our still

                     when the house is paused and

each object seems to tilt in mid-plummet,

                     each red egg a hatching star in my hair,

each surface of my life a border and singularity:

                     the migrant heart sliced into petals by guitar string—

born on a cusp, my first cry erupts

                     a strand of throated river rope

that hangs the crossing in a tissue of fog;

                     in that valley, babies lift to midheaven in sleep, hang

above the deepening cleft, fractaling:

                     a concurrent unweaving as I weave,

the text an unraveling ghost-skirt

                     ever-repeating its leaving and leaving and leaving;

              [*singularity: misterio doloroso*]

in age, after fate will have made an opus

                     of every brutal abandoning

I will succumb to the hunter in the profound:

                                a gallant leap into a copse of pines, the beast

born split, each arrow pierces two beings:

                                in wound, the animal turns constellation;

the feminine, obscene.

# ACKNOWLEDGEMENTS

For publishing poems from this collection, in their many different versions, my deepest gratitude goes to the following publications and their editors:

*Apogee*
*Bettering American Poetry*
*DIAGRAM*
*DREGINALD*
*The Feminist Wire*
*PBS Newshour*
*Pinwheel*
*Poor Claudia*
*Sporklet*
*The Wanderer*
*Waxwing*
*The Western Humanities Review*

I am hugely indebted to the editors and staff at Noemi Press and Letras Latinas, especially Carmen Gimenez Smith, Suzi F. Garcia, Marcelo Hernandez Castillo, and Sarah Gzemski. Thank you for seeing something in this book all the way back in 2015, before it became what it is. Without your brilliance, creative guidance, generosity, and direction, this book would not exist.

To my first mentor, Marcia Douglas, whose embodied, muscular prose challenges the colonial constraints of form and summons ancestral energies—thank you for the permission you gave me to explore this book without expectations in its earliest stages, and for giving me the gift of Audre Lorde's concept of the biomythography as its spiritual guide.

To my mentor and friend, Ruth Ellen Kocher—thank you for your rigor, your genius, and your friendship, and for giving me the eyes to see myself as a poet. Thank you for every opportunity, every extra hour in your office, every check-in, every push you gave me to unearth the radical language I was hiding. Thank you for your shining excellence in the face of institutional and systemic cruelty, for me and every student of color after.

To the Front Range writing community, a special thanks to Khadijah Queen and Carolina Ebeid, as well as Jeffrey Pethybridge, Sommer Browning, Mathias Svalina, Elisa Gabbert, Julie Carr and Tim Roberts, Stephen Graham Jones, Noah Eli Gordon, Elisabeth Sheffield and Jeffrey DeShell for holding space for the community. I am also grateful to dear cohort friends Monica Koenig, Hector Ramirez, Adam Bishop, Courtney Morgan, Tanner Hadfield, Gabrielle Lucille Fuentes, Caroline Davidson, Michael Shirzadian, Liz McGehee, Kolby Harvey, Kathleen J. Woods, Ansley Clark, Loie Merritt, and many more who read and believed in these poems early on.

Special gratitude to Muriel Leung, whose empathy, character, work ethic, and kindness I admire—thank you for looking after me, and for sharing many meals in this lonely city.

Shout out to L.A. and the incredible organizers, friends, and activists holding space for marginalized communities to tell their stories: Pauline Gloss and Spoken Records, Xochitl Julisa Bermejo and Women Who Submit, Cathy Linh Che and Kundiman L.A., Kenji Liu and Vickie Vertiz, F. Douglas Brown, Soraya Membreno, Karineh Mahdessian, Jessica Ceballos Campbell and everyone at Avenue 50 Studio, Neelanjanah Banerjee and Kaya Press, Jen Hofer and everyone at Antena, Jean Ho and Diana Arterian, Sam Cohen and everyone at Yes Femmes, Chiwan Choi, Joseph Rios, Poetic Research Bureau, Eastside Café, CIELO Galleries, Human Resources, A Gathering of Latina Writers, and the organizers and readers at Writers Resist L.A. at Beyond Baroque—thank you all for your urgent work and for welcoming me into your communities.

Huge gratitude to the CantoMundo community, especially Deborah Paredez, Celeste Guzman Mendoza, Carmen Tafolla, and Norma Cantú—thank you for your vision and your tireless labor on behalf of Latinx writers. Thank you for holding space so that Latinx writers can feel seen, and heard, and held, and at home. Without this community and its care, this book would not exist.

More friends, exemplars, and chosen family, thank you for reading this in its many stages, for our conversations, for co-organizing, for your beautiful support: Derrick Austin, Suzi F. Garcia and Rob Bruno, Marcelo Hernandez Castillo and Rubi Hernandez who I must thank again (and again), Jennif(f)er Tamayo, Raquel Salas Rivera, Natalie Scenters Zapico, Carina Del Valle Schorske, Tim Jones Yelvington, Joey De Jesus, Raquel Gutiérrez, Naima Yael Tokunow, Lara Mimosa Montes, Safiya Sinclair, and Eduardo Martinez Leyva.

Every gratitude in this world goes to mis papás, Silvia Angelica Villarreal y Gilberto Villarreal, whose courage, love, and strength astounds me every day. Thank you for your immeasurable sacrifice, for your fight, for your survival. *El árbol empieza aquí.* To mi hermano, Gilbert Villarreal, thank you for your joy and your brilliant creativity, you will make it. And to my family—Tia Mela, Tio Samuel, Tio Joel, Tia Luisa, Tia Ana, Wendy, Carlitos, Willy, Angélica, Ivette, Miriam, Liz, Ileanita, Doris, Adriana, and many many more, I treasure every memory I have of you, and wish every day to go back to tiempos viejos with you all. Thank you. Los quiero, y los extraño.

As always, my work would not be possible without the love and support of my partner and husband, Jesse Johnson. Little Joaquín, light of my life, you pushed this book out into the world with you. Kona and Raja, best beasts. Thank you to my little family.

This book is written in memoriam of my elders and their incredible survival, and against every attempt to overwrite or erase their stories.

Angélica—until we meet again.